HOPE FOR RYAN WHITE

DANO MORENO

ILLUSTRATED BY
HANNAH ABBO

ALBERT WHITMAN & COMPANY
CHICAGO, ILLINOIS

For Ryan—DM

To Luis and Joao, all my love—HA

Library of Congress Cataloging-in-Publication data is on file with the publisher.
Text copyright © 2023 by Dano Moreno
Illustrations copyright © 2023 by Albert Whitman & Company
Illustrations by Hannah Abbo
First published in the United States of America
in 2023 by Albert Whitman & Company
ISBN 978-0-8075-3354-3 (hardcover)
ISBN 978-0-8075-3355-0 (ebook)

Printed in China
10 9 8 7 6 5 4 3 2 1 WKT 26 25 24 23 22

Design by Mary Freelove

For more information about Albert Whitman & Company,
visit our website at www.albertwhitman.com.

It was Christmas Day 1984. Ryan White had imagined he'd be at home in Kokomo, Indiana. Instead, he was in a hospital in Indianapolis.

He had been so sick that his doctor sent him there earlier that month. Ryan was starting to feel better. And seeing his room packed with people and presents, he couldn't help but smile.

His mom and his sister, Andrea, returned the next day.

Mom had been working up the courage to tell Ryan his diagnosis from the doctor. "Ryan," she said softly. "You have AIDS."

Ryan was stunned.

He had seen the news. AIDS was a new disease caused by a virus that infected people's blood. When people with AIDS got sick, they had trouble recovering. There was no cure and no good medicine to treat it. People were dying from AIDS. Many were gay men.

Those were facts. But misinformation was spreading too. Some people thought you could get AIDS from doorknobs or toilet seats. Others thought only gay men could get it. Some even believed that people with AIDS had done something wrong.

Ryan knew better.

And he knew the reason he had AIDS: Ryan was born with a
condition called hemophilia. This meant his body needed help to stop
bleeding when he got a bruise or a cut. For his body to heal, Ryan
needed treatments made from donated blood. But the treatments that
had kept him alive had also made him sick.

The doctor didn't know how long Ryan would live. Maybe months. Maybe years.

Ryan worried he'd spend the rest of his life in the hospital. He worried he'd never see his friends again—or grow old enough to drive a car.

As the days passed, his fear faded. And after a month, Ryan felt well enough to go home.

After a few more months, Ryan felt well enough to go to school.

Doctors and other experts were certain that Ryan couldn't give AIDS to anyone else by playing or sitting with them. Yet his classmates' parents and school officials believed he could. Instead of listening to experts, they talked with each other.

Misinformation echoed through town. The more the lies were repeated, the more they seemed true.

"They're afraid you'll infect the other kids," said Mom.

"But that's impossible!" Ryan replied. "I want to be with my friends, just like everybody else."

When reporters heard that Ryan wasn't allowed in class because he had AIDS, they came to interview him.

Ryan wanted people to get to know him—to see that he wasn't a threat. "I understand why the school is scared," he said calmly. "But they should just listen to the facts."

The next morning, people across the country watched Ryan on TV. For most of them, it was their first time seeing a kid with AIDS. Ryan's courage was inspiring—and many began to question their beliefs.

Still, others refused to accept him, especially in Kokomo. People started rumors that Ryan was gay—and trying to spread AIDS to others. None of this was true.

When Ryan wasn't in the
hospital, he was lonely at home.

Mom found a lawyer who wanted to help get Ryan back in school. They went to court again and again—and argued that Ryan had a right to be in class. Each time, others argued he didn't. It felt like a battle that would never end.

Reporters made sure Ryan stayed in the news. Throughout the country and across the globe, people watched and rooted for him. They even wrote him letters.

But in town, people acted as if they wished he'd disappear. They stared and whispered. And they wouldn't touch him.

Ryan's lawyer asked if he wanted to stop going to court.

"No!" Ryan replied. "We're right. They're wrong."

Ryan was determined to make things better—not just for himself, but for all people with AIDS. If he was kept out of school, surely others would be too. He couldn't let that happen.

After a year in and out of court...

He won!

The court's decision sent a message: classrooms are for everyone. Ryan smiled from ear to ear.

His victory made headlines. Ryan traveled to speak on TV shows.
He helped celebrities raise money for AIDS research. Like them, Ryan
had become famous too.

But back at school, kids avoided him. Adults told them to stay away. It was clear that Ryan *still* wasn't welcome. He was lonelier than ever—and desperate for a fresh start.

In the summer of 1987, Ryan and his family moved to Cicero, Indiana—a small town less than an hour away.

One day, after settling into their new home, the doorbell rang. Ryan was sure it was a reporter.

It wasn't.

"Hi, Ryan. I'm Jill Stewart. I live two doors down from you."

Jill was the student body president at Ryan's new high school.

"Now you'll know someone on your first day at school."

Jill kept visiting throughout the summer. Finally, Ryan had friends again. Finally, he was happy. Still, he wondered how others would treat him when school started.

Jill did too.

She talked with school officials, and they hatched a plan. They invited experts to visit and answer questions about AIDS.

Then students became teachers in their homes. They explained
to their parents that they couldn't get AIDS from being around Ryan.

Conversations about AIDS echoed through town—conversations led by kids and based on facts. The more people knew, the less they feared.

When his first day arrived, Ryan worried that the school's plan wouldn't work—that his classmates would be cruel.

As the car pulled up, a voice called out, "There he is!"

Uh-oh, thought Ryan.

He walked toward the school and saw reporters waiting for him. He expected that. But others were waiting too...

Ryan beamed. With friends at his side, he felt excited to go to school again.

He felt something else too...

Hope that there must be more kids like the ones standing by him.

And hope that, together, they could change the world.

HOW RYAN CHANGED THE WORLD

After winning his case and moving to a different town, Ryan White continued to speak up. And the world listened. Ryan inspired countless people to be brave, to be inclusive, and to learn about AIDS and HIV, the virus that causes AIDS. He even helped educate teachers and lawmakers.

Ryan lived until age eighteen. Shortly after he died in 1990, Congress passed the Ryan White Comprehensive AIDS Resources Emergency (CARE) Act, creating programs that provided medicine and support for people with HIV throughout the United States. These programs live on today, helping hundreds of thousands of people. We can all honor Ryan by sharing his story, listening to experts, and spreading facts instead of fear.

ANSWERING QUESTIONS ABOUT HIV AND AIDS

How does HIV affect the body?

Inside our bodies, our immune systems fight off infections and help us stay healthy. When HIV gets in the body, it attacks the immune system. Without medicine to fight the virus, HIV can weaken the immune system, causing AIDS and other serious health problems.

How do people get HIV?

Every virus is different. HIV lives in blood, breast milk, and some other body fluids. You can only get HIV if the virus gets inside your body. Ryan White got HIV because his hemophilia treatments were made from other people's blood. Some of the donated blood contained HIV and was injected into his body. This was in the early 1980s, before a test had been invented to check for HIV in blood. Today, all donated blood in the United States is tested for HIV. If blood is found to have HIV, it is not given to others.

What are some things that *don't* spread HIV?

HIV does not spread through saliva, sweat, tears, skin, the air, or mosquitoes. That means you cannot get HIV from someone by playing with them, shaking hands, hugging, sharing food or drinks, or sitting on a toilet seat.

How has the HIV epidemic changed?

Today, fewer people are getting HIV, and we have more hope than ever. Because of new and better medicines, many people with HIV now live long lives without ever developing AIDS. Some of the same medicines also stop HIV from being passed on to others. Every day, people are working hard to end the epidemic—to create a future where everyone with HIV is healthy and there are no new infections.